8.99

Three Weel

CANCELLED 2009

London: The Stationery Office

Researched and written by Publishing Services, Central Office of Information.

© Crown copyright material reproduced under licence from the Controller of Her Majesty's Stationery Office and the Central Office of Information 1997
Applications for reproduction should be made to Crown Copyright Unit, St Clements House, 2-16 Colegate, Norwich NR3 1BQ
First published 1991
Second edition 1997
ISBN 0 11 701980 1

Published by The Stationery Office and available from:

The Publications Centre
(mail, telephone and fax orders only)
PO Box 276, London SW8 5DT
General enquiries 0171 873 0011
Telephone orders 0171 873 9090
Fax orders 0171 873 8200

The Stationery Office Bookshops
49 High Holborn, London WC1V 6HB
(counter service and fax orders only) Fax 0171 831 1326
68-69 Bull Street, Birmingham B4 6AD 0121 236 9696 Fax 0121 236 9699
33 Wine Street, Bristol BS1 2BQ 01179 264306 Fax 01179 294515
9-21 Princess Street, Manchester M60 8AS 0161 834 7201 Fax 0161 833 0634
16 Arthur Street, Belfast BT1 4GD 0123 223 8451 Fax 0123 223 5401
The Stationery Office Oriel Bookshop,
The Friary, Cardiff CF1 4AA 01222 395548 Fax 01222 384347
71 Lothian Road, Edinburgh EH3 9AZ (counter service only)

Customers in Scotland may mail, telephone or fax their orders to:
Scottish Publication Sales,
South Gyle Crescent, Edinburgh EH12 9EB 0131 479 3141 Fax 0131 479 3142

Accredited Agents (see Yellow Pages)

and through good booksellers

Contents

Acknowledgments

This book has been compiled with the help of a number of organisations. The Central Office of Information would like to thank in particular the Home Office, the Department for Education and Employment, the Departments of the Environment and Health, the Northern Ireland Office, The Scottish Office, the Office for National Statistics, the Commission for Racial Equality and the BBC.

Autumn 1996

Introduction

The most notable social change in Britain[1] in the period after the Second World War has been the settlement of substantial immigrant communities, mainly from former colonies in the Caribbean and the South Asian sub-continent (Bangladesh, India and Pakistan). Migrant workers were similarly attracted to most other industrialised Western European countries. The 1991 Census returns show that Britain is now a multiracial society with a non-White ethnic minority population of about 3 million—5.5 per cent of the total population—of whom almost a half were born in Britain.

Arriving in the 1950s and 1960s the new immigrants settled in the inner cities where, at the time, employment opportunities were greatest and housing was cheapest. The economic base of these areas was already declining, however, leaving many members of the Black and Asian communities disproportionately concentrated in areas of greatest deprivation and social stress. In some instances ethnic minorities have also faced racial discrimination in employment, housing, and health and social services. During the early to mid-1980s some of these areas were the scene of urban disorders, highlighting a breakdown in confidence between the police and certain members of the community, both Black and White.

However, successive British governments have been

[1] The term 'Britain' is used informally in this book to mean the United Kingdom of Great Britain and Northern Ireland. 'Great Britain' comprises England, Scotland and Wales.

committed to the principles of equality before the law and equality of opportunity. Legislation has made discrimination unlawful in employment, education, housing and the provision of goods and services, and policies are being pursued to promote equality of opportunity for all citizens. Extensive efforts have been made to combat racial disadvantage through the social, economic, educational and environmental programmes of central and local government, which have channelled substantial expenditure into the regeneration of the inner cities. Measures have also been taken to involve local people more closely in deciding on priorities and on targeting funds more effectively.

Much progress has been made over the last 25 years, and ethnic minority communities now make a large, positive contribution to the social, economic and cultural well-being of Britain. Although members of the ethnic minorities increasingly participate in all areas of national life, many others continue to lack the opportunity to overcome the disadvantages they experience. Nevertheless, much enterprise is being shown by Black and Asian people to improve the well-being of their communities. Policies for tackling the problems of the inner cities are designed to encourage self-help and voluntary action in creating a greater sense of community. Moreover, a growing number of institutions, including local authorities, public bodies, companies and trade unions, are taking stronger action to ensure that opportunities are equally available to all.

This book outlines some of the action being taken by the Government and others to combat disadvantage, including measures in education and employment, the health and social services, and housing. Reference is made to the action being taken to improve relations between the police and ethnic communities.

There is also a description of the press and the broadcasting services for the ethnic minorities and their activities in the arts.

On the question of terminology, while many ethnic minority people prefer to use the all-embracing word 'Black', in certain contexts it is more helpful to distinguish between Black and Asian groups. The latter course has been taken in this book where a distinction is relevant. Even so, within these broad groups are people from a diversity of religions, languages and cultural backgrounds.

Immigration and Demographic Trends

Because of its long tradition of accommodating immigrants and refugees and because it is part of a multiracial Commonwealth, Britain contains a diversity of people. In London students and business people from overseas add to the number of nationalities resident there and the city is among the most multicultural in the world. It has been estimated that about 160 languages and dialects are spoken in London schools.

For many centuries British society has absorbed immigrants and refugees seeking better economic opportunities or escaping political or religious persecution. They have included Huguenots (Protestants) from France in the 17th century, Jews from the European continent and Irish immigrants. Refugees from Nazi Germany arrived in the 1930s. After the Second World War, refugees and displaced people from Eastern Europe, Poles in particular and subsequently Hungarians, entered Britain.

The presence of some Black immigrants was recorded in the 16th century. In the 17th and 18th centuries young Black people were brought to Britain as domestic servants. Former slaves from the Caribbean followed, and Black seamen have traditionally settled in ports such as Liverpool, Bristol and Cardiff.

Substantial immigration from the Caribbean, India, Pakistan and Bangladesh[2] began in the 1950s. Migrant workers were

[2]Pakistan formerly consisted of two separate states—East and West Pakistan. In 1971 East Pakistan became the new state of Bangladesh.

also attracted to most other industrialised Western European countries at this time. In addition, in 1972, Britain admitted some 28,000 Asians expelled from Uganda and, since the late 1970s, has admitted some 22,000 refugees from South-East Asia. Chinese immigration developed in the 19th century with seamen settling in London and Liverpool. It continued after the Second World War and accelerated, especially from Hong Kong, in the 1960s. Significant numbers of Italians, Greek and Turkish Cypriots, Australians, New Zealanders and people from the United States and Canada are also resident in Britain.

Black people came to Britain from the widely scattered islands in the Caribbean which are now in the Commonwealth, as well as from the mainland territories of Guyana and Belize. Nearly 60 per cent of these came from Jamaica. Although they share a colonial history, the people of each island regard themselves as distinctive from the others. Their mother tongue is English, although a variety of dialects are spoken, and they adhere mainly to Christian denominations. In the 1950s and 1960s job opportunities were better in Britain than in their own countries and some of those who came had served in the Royal Air Force during the Second World War or had worked as skilled craftsmen in factories on Merseyside. Others were recruited to work in London on the buses and the underground railway system.

Immigration from India and Pakistan (including Bangladesh), which began later than that from the Caribbean, reached its peak in the late 1960s, prompted by a desire for better opportunities in employment—especially in the textile industry—and education. Large numbers of people migrating from Pakistan and Bangladesh continued throughout the 1970s and into the

1980s. The Bangladeshi migration is the more recent, with over one-third arriving in Britain in the 1980s.

Most Indians have come from the Punjab and Gujarat. Their languages include Punjabi, Gujarati, Urdu and Hindi. Many of those of Asian origin from East Africa are also Gujarati, mainly descended from Indians who migrated there as businessmen or to work in railway construction. Those who came to Britain from Bangladesh speak Bengali. Religious groupings cross the national divisions. While Muslims, Hindus and Sikhs are the most numerous, the Asian community also includes Christians.

In recent years, the number of people coming from the Asian sub-continent has remained roughly constant, but there has been a rise in the number of people from African countries such as Ghana, Nigeria and Somalia as a result of the increase in asylum applications.

Immigration Controls

Until 1962 Commonwealth citizens had always been free to enter Britain as they wished. In that year, however, the Government decided to limit the number of immigrants to a level the country could absorb, both economically and socially, and the first legislation to control Commonwealth immigration was passed. Further restrictions were introduced in 1968, and entry from all countries is now controlled by the Immigration Act 1971 (as amended by the Immigration Act 1988 and the Asylum and Immigration Appeals Act 1993), which is administered under immigration rules made in accordance with the Act.

Reflecting these restrictions, the overall level of immigration has been decreasing. Recent settlement totals remain markedly lower than in the mid-1970s: 55,000 in 1994 compared with

82,000 in 1975. The majority of those accepted for settlement are spouses or dependants of people who are British citizens, or who are settled or settling in this country. In recent years, around a half of those accepted were wives and children, and a further one-fifth were husbands. Of the total accepted for settlement in 1994, 33,000 (59 per cent) were citizens of the Commonwealth; 22,000 (41 per cent) were from other countries.

Asylum

In recent years there has been a significant increase in the numbers of people seeking asylum in Britain and other European countries. Britain has passed legislation strengthening safeguards for genuine refugees but reducing the scope for others to misuse the asylum process. All asylum cases are assessed in accordance with the criteria set out in the 1951 United Nations Convention relating to the Status of Refugees.[3]

Numbers and Demographic Characteristics

The most comprehensive statistics on ethnic minority populations come from the 1991 Census of Population, which for the first time included a question on ethnic origin.[4] The ethnic group classifications in the 1991 Census question were White, Black Caribbean, Black African, Black Other (often aggregated into a single 'Black' category for statistical purposes), Indian, Pakistani, Bangladeshi, Chinese, and an Any Other category.

The 1991 Census found that 94.5 per cent of the population belonged to the White group, while just over 3 million (5.5 per cent) described themselves as belonging to another ethnic group

[3]For further information see *Human Rights* (Aspects of Britain: HMSO, 1996).
[4]For further information see *Population* (Aspects of Britain: HMSO, 1995).

(see Table 1). Most (97 per cent) of those classified as members of an ethnic minority lived in England, while 2 per cent lived in Scotland and 1.4 per cent in Wales. In England ethnic minority groups made up 6.2 per cent of the population, in Scotland 1.3 per cent and in Wales 1.5 per cent. The largest of the minority groups in England was Indian (28 per cent of the total), followed by Black Caribbeans (17 per cent) and Pakistanis (15 per cent). The smallest ethnic category identified from the Census overall was the Chinese, but this group was relatively much larger in Scotland (17 per cent) and in Wales (12 per cent) than in England (4.9 per cent).

Table 1: Resident Population by Ethnic Group in Great Britain, 1991

Ethnic group	All persons ('000)	Percentage born in Britain	Percentage of total population
White	51,874	96	94.5
All ethnic minority groups	3,015	47	5.5
Black groups	891	56	1.6
Black Caribbean	500	54	0.9
Black African	212	36	0.4
Black other	178	85	0.3
Indian	840	42	1.5
Pakistani	477	51	0.9
Bangladeshi	163	37	0.3
Chinese	157	29	0.3
Other groups	488	44	0.9
All groups	54,889	93	100

Source: 1991 Census
Note: Differences between totals and sums of their component parts are due to rounding.

Figure 1: Population by Ethnic Minority Group (Women and Men)

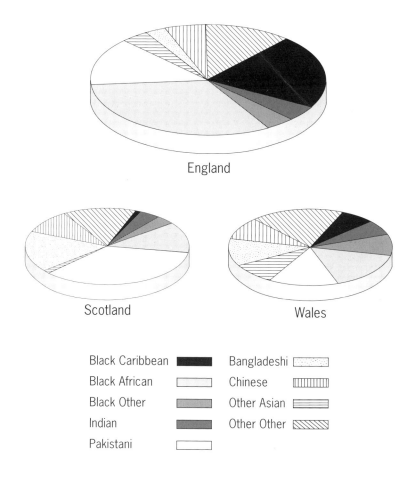

England

Scotland

Wales

Black Caribbean	■	Bangladeshi	
Black African		Chinese	
Black Other		Other Asian	
Indian		Other Other	
Pakistani			

Source: *Black and Ethnic Minority Women and Men*
Equal Opportunities Commission.

Table 2: Population by Ethnic Group and Region, 1991

Thousands and percentages

	Black[a]	Indian, Pakistani or Bangladeshi	Other ethnic minority groups	All ethnic minority groups	White	All ethnic groups	Ethnic minority groups as a percentage of total population
Great Britain	891	1,480	645	3,015	51,874	54,889	5.5
North	5	21	13	39	2,988	3,027	1.3
Yorkshire & Humberside	37	144	33	214	4,623	4,837	4.4
East Midlands	39	120	29	188	3,765	3,953	4.8
East Anglia	14	14	15	43	1,984	2,027	2.1
South East	610	691	395	1,695	15,513	17,208	9.9
Greater London	535	521	290	1,346	5,334	6,680	20.2
Rest of South East	74	170	104	349	10,179	10,529	3.3
South West	22	17	24	63	4,547	4,609	1.4
West Midlands	102	277	45	424	4,726	5,150	8.2
North West	47	147	50	245	5,999	6,244	3.9
England	875	1,431	605	2,911	44,144	47,055	6.2
Wales	9	16	16	42	2,794	2,835	1.5
Scotland	6	32	24	63	4,936	4,999	1.3

Source: Office of Population Censuses and Surveys[5]: General Register Office (Scotland)

[a]Black Caribbean, Black African and Black Other

Note: Differences between totals and sums of their component parts are due to rounding.

[5]In 1996 the Office of Population Censuses and Surveys merged with the Central Statistical Office to form the Office for National Statistics.

Distribution

According to the 1991 Census, ethnic minority communities were concentrated in metropolitan and industrial areas; 45 per cent lived in Greater London, compared with only 10 per cent of the White population. In nine London boroughs, ethnic minority groups accounted for over 25 per cent of the population, with the highest proportion (45 per cent) in Brent; the Bangladeshi group alone made up 23 per cent of the population of Tower Hamlets.

In all, about three-fifths (60 per cent) of the people from Black ethnic groups lived in Greater London, compared with about two-fifths (41 per cent) of Indians and just under one-fifth (18 per cent) of Pakistanis.

Outside the capital, there were high concentrations of ethnic minority populations in Leicester and Slough (both 28 per cent) and in Birmingham (22 per cent). In Leicester, the Indian group comprised over three-quarters of the ethnic minority population, whereas Pakistanis were the largest component in Birmingham (32 per cent), and were also concentrated in the Yorkshire and Lancashire textile towns of Bradford, Rochdale and Blackburn, and in Luton.

Ethnic minorities in Scotland numbered about 62,000 and their greatest concentration was in Glasgow, Edinburgh, Aberdeen and Dundee. The largest ethnic group was the Pakistani group (21,000). In Wales the majority lived in Cardiff and Newport.

There are no precise figures for the number of members of ethnic minority groups in Northern Ireland, since the question on ethnicity was not asked in the 1991 Census there. From surveys it is estimated that the largest group is the Chinese community, with about 8,000 members. Other Asian minorities originate from Bangladesh, India and Pakistan. There are also the traditional Irish Travellers, who share some of the characteristics of an ethnic minority.

Overall, nearly half of the ethnic minority population was born in Britain, although this proportion varies from group to group (see Table 3). There has been relatively little immigration in recent years; as a consequence, only 14 per cent of the under-16 age group recorded in the *Labour Force Survey*[6] in 1994 were born abroad, compared with almost three-quarters of the working age population. In the case of Indians 93 per cent of children were born in Britain, compared with 98 per cent of White children. At the other end of the spectrum, virtually all people of ethnic minority groups over the age of 35 were born abroad, although the percentage is less for Black people (94 per cent).

Age Structure and Household Characteristics

Ethnic minority groups have a far younger age structure than the White population. At the 1991 Census about one-third (32 per cent) of the people belonging to ethnic minorities were under the age of 16, compared with one-fifth (20 per cent) of the population of Great Britain as a whole. Only 3 per cent of ethnic minority groups were over the age of 65, compared with 16 per cent of Great Britain's population as a whole.

According to the 1991 Census, well over half of all Pakistani households (54 per cent) and Bangladeshi households (62 per cent) had five or more residents, compared with less than one in ten (7 per cent) of White households. Pakistani and Bangladeshi

[6]The *Labour Force Survey* is a quarterly survey of about 60,000 households. It includes questions about ethnic origin and country of birth.

households also had the largest number of children, with over half of Bangladeshi households having three or more children.

Official surveys show that in early 1994, 29 per cent of White households were single-person households, compared with 31 per cent of Black households and a much lower 7 per cent of Pakistani/Bangladeshi households. Households headed by a Pakistani or Bangladeshi were most likely to contain dependent children. The high proportion of White single person households is attributable to elderly people being more likely to live alone and the White population having an older age distribution than that for ethnic minority groups. There are also cultural differences: for example, over half of Black Caribbean mothers were lone mothers in 1989–91 compared with just over one in ten Pakistani/Bangladeshi mothers.

Table 3: People Born Outside Britain by Ethnic Origin and Age, Spring 1994 *Percentage*

Age group	All origins	White	Ethnic minority groups				
			All	Black	Indian	Pakistani/ Bangladeshi	Mixed/ other origins
All ages	7	4	54	48	59	54	56
0–15	3	2	14	15	7	16	18
16–24	6	4	40	24	28	52	51
25–34	9	5	65	40	77	83	74
35–44	10	5	94	84	99	98	94
45–59/64	8	5	98	99	100	100	94
16–59/64	9	5	73	59	78	79	76
60/65 & over	7	5	100	100	99	100	100

Source: Labour Force Survey

Ethnic Minorities in Society

Members of ethnic minorities may experience more social disadvantages than other groups. Their children may be more likely to need special help in education, and unemployment is higher among the ethnic minorities. Such difficulties have in the past been compounded by unfamiliarity with British society and, especially among some Asian groups, by differences in language and culture. Social disadvantage may also be aggravated by racial discrimination.

The commitment of successive governments has been to promote equality of opportunity and to eradicate discrimination. The main economic, social, educational and environmental programmes are designed to bring about improvements in many of the inner city areas. Special measures have been taken to help with difficulties arising, for example, out of language and cultural differences and to give help to the unemployed. Legislation against discrimination was first introduced in 1965. Its scope was widened by the Race Relations Act 1968, which made discrimination in employment, housing and education, and in the provision of goods, facilities and services, unlawful. The law was further strengthened by the Race Relations Act 1976 (see p. 19).

Ethnic Monitoring

The collection and examination of statistical information on ethnic origin by employers and those providing services is an important means of checking whether equal opportunity policies are being put into practice effectively. The results of monitoring can be used to establish equal opportunities targets (as distinct from quotas), and to show the extent to which these are met. On a national level, the ethnic origin information derived from the 1991 Census of Population helps central and local government and health authorities to allocate resources and plan programmes, taking account of the needs of each ethnic group.

Ethnic monitoring practices have been adopted by the Civil Service (see p. 51), the National Health Service (NHS), the armed services and the criminal justice agencies, including the police, probation service, prison service, Crown Prosecution Service and courts' services. The Home Secretary is required to publish annually statistical information relating to treatment of ethnic minorities in the criminal justice system.

Religious Beliefs and Practices

Everyone in Britain has the right to religious freedom without interference from the community or the state. Religious organisations and groups may own property, conduct their rites and ceremonies, run schools and promote their beliefs in speech and writing within the limits of the law. There is a wide variety of religious beliefs and traditions, although a substantial proportion of ethnic minority members also belong to Christian denominations.

The Muslim Community

Figures for the size of the Muslim population in Britain have ranged from three-quarters of a million to 2 million. Recent estimates, based on extrapolations from the 1991 Census, suggest the population is between 1 million and 1.5 million, while estimates from within the Muslim community suggest between 1.5 and 2 million. Most originate from Pakistan and Bangladesh, while sizeable groups have come from India, Cyprus, the Arab world, Malaysia and parts of Africa.

There are some 600 mosques and numerous Muslim prayer centres throughout Britain. One of the most important Muslim institutions in the Western world is the Central Mosque in London and its associated Islamic Cultural Centre. The Central Mosque has the largest congregation in Britain, and during festivals it may number over' 30,000. There are also important mosques and cultural centres in Liverpool, Manchester, Leicester, Birmingham, Bradford, Cardiff, Edinburgh and Glasgow.

Many of the mosques are administered by various local Muslim organisations, and both Sunni and Shi'a traditions within Islam are represented among British Muslims. Branches of some of the major Sufi traditions have been established in British cities. The Ismaili Centre in London provides wide-ranging pastoral care and a place of worship for Shi'a Imami Ismaili Muslims, whose current Imam is Prince Karim Aga Khan.

Muslims have also formed many national and local organisations, mainly concerned with religious, educational, social and welfare activities.

The Sikh Community

There is a large Sikh community, comprising an estimated 400,000 to 500,000 people. Most came from the Punjab in north-west India, although a large minority have come via East Africa. The largest groups of Sikhs are in Greater London, Manchester, Birmingham, Nottingham and Wolverhampton.

Over 200 Sikh temples cater for the religious, educational,

social welfare and cultural needs of their community. The oldest central temple in London was established in 1908 and the largest is in Hounslow, Middlesex.

The Hindu Community

There are about 320,000 Hindus in Britain, originating largely from the Indian provinces of Gujarat and Punjab. The community is one of the most recent of the South Asian communities to develop in Britain. Some Hindus arrived directly from India in the 1950s and early 1960s, but most, although of Indian origin, came from East Africa in the late 1960s and early 1970s. Some, again of Indian origin, have come from other parts of the world, including Fiji and Trinidad. The largest groups of Hindus are to be found in Leicester, different areas of London, Birmingham and Bradford.

Large numbers of Hindus, although not required to attend a place of worship regularly, attend Hindu temples for annual festivals. The first Hindu temple, or *mandir*, was opened in London in 1962 and there are now over 150, a number of which are affiliated to the National Council of Hindu Temples, and to the Vishwa Hindu Parishad, which is an international organisation. The Swaminarayan Hindu Mission in north London has the largest Hindu temple to be built outside India, together with an extensive cultural complex with provision for conferences, exhibitions, marriage ceremonies, sports and health clinics.

Other Religious Groups

Other religious persuasions include about 30,000 Jains, whose religion is of ancient Indian origin. A *deresar*, or Jain temple, opened in Leicester in 1988. The Zoroastrian religion, or

Mazdaism, which originated in ancient Iran, is mainly represented in Britain by the Parsi community, whose ancestors left Iran in the tenth century and settled in north-west India. The Baha'i movement originates from Iran; there are an estimated 6,000 Baha'is in Britain, organised in 500 local assemblies and administered by the National Spiritual Assembly in London. Rastafarianism, which grew out of the Back to Africa movement in the West Indies, has attracted support among the Black Caribbean population.

Co-operation between Faiths
The Inter Faith Network for the United Kingdom is one of several organisations which seek to develop relations between different religions in Britain. It links a wide range of organisations, including representative bodies from the Baha'i, Buddhist, Christian, Hindu, Jain, Jewish, Muslim, Sikh and Zoroastrian faith groups.

Race Relations Legislation

Policies to remove racial disadvantage and to promote equality of opportunity are pursued against a background of legislation against racial discrimination. The Race Relations Act 1976, which applies to England, Scotland and Wales, makes racial discrimination generally unlawful in a wide range of circumstances.

Following a process of public consultation, the Government is to introduce legislation for Northern Ireland on the lines of the Race Relations Act 1976.

Definition of Discrimination

Under the Act, two kinds of conduct are racially discriminatory:

—'direct discrimination', which means treating a person less favourably on grounds of colour, race, nationality, or ethnic or national origins; and

—'indirect discrimination', which is treatment that may be described as 'equal in a formal sense as between different racial groups, but discriminatory in its effect on one particular racial group'.

The Act makes racial discrimination unlawful:

—in employment, including recruitment, terms and conditions of work, training, promotion and dismissal;

—in education;

—in the provision of goods, facilities and services; and

—in the disposal and management of premises.

It is also unlawful to pursue 'discriminatory practices' in which indirect discrimination may occur although there is no identifiable victim. Such practices may include discriminatory advertisements, instructions or pressure to discriminate or aiding discrimination. Segregation on racial grounds is regarded as racial discrimination. The Act makes it unlawful for clubs and associations of 25 members or more to discriminate in the selection of new members. It also places a duty on local authorities to carry out their functions in such a way that discrimination is eliminated and equality of opportunity and good race relations promoted.

There are a number of general exceptions to the Act: for example, for employment in a private household or in order to meet the needs of a particular racial group in education, training or welfare.

The Act does not permit 'reverse discrimination'. This means discrimination in favour of a person of a particular racial group, for example, in recruitment or promotion, on the grounds that members of that group have in the past suffered from adverse discrimination. It does, however, permit certain forms of 'positive action' in particular circumstances. That may take the form of training and encouragement of people of a particular racial group to take advantage of opportunities for doing work in which they are under-represented. It may not be unlawful to discriminate in selection for jobs where membership of a particular racial group is a genuine occupational qualification.

Enforcement

People who consider that they have suffered unlawful discrimination have the right to go to a civil court. Cases involving discrimination in employment, partnerships, trade unions, qualifying bodies and employment agencies are dealt with by an industrial tribunal. It is unlawful to victimise people asserting their rights under the 1976 Act.

If a person goes to court, the remedies available are:

—the award of damages, including damages for injured feelings;

—an order declaring the rights of the parties; or

—an injunction (or order in Scotland) ordering a particular person or body to perform, or not to commit, or to cease committing, specified acts.

An industrial tribunal sends a copy of a complaint concerning discrimination in employment to the independent Advisory, Conciliation and Arbitration Service (ACAS), which helps the parties to reach a settlement without the need for a tribunal hearing. If the case is heard by a tribunal, it can:

—declare the rights of the parties;

—recommend that the respondent takes a particular course of action; and

—require the respondent to pay the complainant compensation, which may include damages for loss of earnings or injured feelings.

The Race Relations (Remedies) Act 1994 removed the ceiling on compensation awards that industrial tribunals can make in racial discrimination cases.

Commission for Racial Equality

The independent Commission for Racial Equality (CRE) was set up by the 1976 Act to work towards the elimination of discrimination, to promote equality of opportunity and good relations between people of different racial groups, and to keep under review the operation of the Act.

The CRE has the power to help individuals bring complaints of discrimination before the courts or industrial tribunals. Such help may include giving advice, seeking a settlement or arranging for legal advice, assistance or representation. A network to assist complainants is also being set up that will include local independent agencies as well as the CRE. In addition, the CRE has sole responsibility for bringing proceedings in connection with discriminatory practices, advertisements and pressure to discriminate, and it has powers to deal with persistent discrimination.

The CRE is also empowered to conduct formal investigations. If it is satisfied that the Act has been contravened, it can issue an enforceable non-discrimination notice on the people concerned. Recent cases include a vehicle hire firm which had discriminated against Black and Asian customers in hiring cars. A non-discrimination notice was issued on the company requiring it to introduce a comprehensive equal policy covering both the hiring of vehicles and employment practices. In another case, a notice was served on a horticultural club because one of its rules, restricting membership to those who could find a proposer and a seconder within the existing membership, was found to be indirectly discriminatory. Although the club was in an area where the ethnic minority population was nearly 60 per cent, all the club's members were White.

In general, however, the CRE aims to use formal investigations as a weapon of last resort and, instead, persuade employers and organisations to enter into voluntary agreements to take action for equality. A number of voluntary agreements have been entered into by public and private sector companies and agencies.

Many of the cases taken by the CRE never reach a tribunal or court hearing but are settled at an earlier stage in the process, with the respondents often acknowledging the need for changes in procedures and attitudes.

Others priorities for action identified by the CRE include:

—developing racial equality standards in employment, local government and youth services and introducing recognition and award schemes;

—working with national and local agencies through campaigns and other local action programmes to support victims and encourage greater tolerance and respect;

—working for the introduction of specific legislation to outlaw racial harassment, producing good practice guidance on case handling and monitoring work developed at community level;

—ensuring that educational institutions and other agencies providing services for young people take full account of young people of all backgrounds; and

—working in partnership with organisations in support of racial equality, including racial equality councils; local authorities; housing associations, the Social Security Benefits Agency and other public sector agencies; and private and public sector employers and their representative bodies such as the

Association of Chief Police Officers, the Police Federation and the Black Police Association.

In 1994 the CRE registered 1,937 applications for assistance, including 1,314 on employment cases and 576 on non-employment cases, and handled successfully 137 litigation cases (see Table 4). Just over a quarter of all applicants in 1994 were in their 30s, while only 22 were under 20 and 54 over 60.

Table 4: Applications to the Commission for Assistance, and Outcome of Cases, 1990–94

	1990	1991	1992	1993	1994
Applications	1,381	1,655	1,557	1,630	1,937
Employment	960	1,203	1,105	1,160	1,314
Non-employment	379	375	412	425	576
Results	85	137	113	210	137
Settled on terms	59	112	87	110[a]	116
Successful after hearing	26	25	26	100[b]	21[c]
Dismissed	24	29	24	26	15

[a] Includes 34 cases settled by complaints officers before the Commission decided to grant legal representation.
[b] Includes 72 individual cases against a single company.
[c] A further 31 were won, several by agencies supported by the Commission.

Codes of Practice

Codes of practice have been issued by the CRE on the elimination of racial discrimination and the promotion of equality of opportunity in employment, housing, education, health care and maternity services. The CRE has also produced a Racial Equality Standard for employers and for local authorities. Its aim is to give employers, especially large employers and service providers, clear guidance on how to build racial equality into their approach as corporate citizens. A similar standard has been developed for the legal authorities. As well as working with other equality agencies, such as the Equal Opportunities Commissions in Britain and Northern Ireland and the Fair Employment Commission in Northern Ireland, the CRE also makes grants to national and local voluntary and self-help organisations concerned with the promotion of equality of opportunity and good race relations.

A recent example of the CRE's partnership approach has been the Let's Kick Racism Out of Football campaign. Launched in 1993 with the Professional Footballers' Association, and with support from the Football Trust, the campaign aimed to ensure that racism in sport was high on the agenda of the media. A decision to take the campaign to young people has led to the production of a free, full-colour magazine *Kick It*, sponsored by the Football Trust.

Financed by a grant from the Home Office, the Commission's expenditure in 1993–94 was £15 million.

Racial Equality Councils

The CRE supports and finances a network of 86 local racial equality councils (RECs). These are voluntary bodies which promote equality of opportunity, good race relations and the elimination of racial discrimination. The councils are usually composed of representatives of statutory and voluntary bodies, including the churches, trade unions, and ethnic minority organisations committed to racial equality.

Many RECs have been involved in local initiatives to help

victims of racially motivated harassment and violence:

—Sutton REC is administering a scheme funded by the local borough which provides ethnic minority residents with an alarm they can set off if harassed;

—Essex REC has worked to develop multi-agency racial incidents panels throughout the county; and

—Greenwich REC is working with Greenwich University in the setting up of a system to monitor racial harassment and attacks on the campus.

About 28 per cent of the CRE's budget was allocated to RECs in grants for employing staff in 1993–94. RECs also receive additional financial assistance from their local government authority to cover projects and administration.

Incitement to Racial Hatred

Under the Public Order Act 1986 it is an offence to use threatening, abusive or insulting words or to publish or distribute material likely to, or intended to, stir up racial hatred. This also applies to behaviour designed to stir up racial hatred. The offence is punishable by a fine and/or imprisonment. In England and Wales a prosecution may be brought only by, or with the consent of, the Attorney-General.

It is also an offence to possess racially inflammatory material with a view to its publication or distribution. The Criminal Justice and Public Order Act 1994 makes publication and distribution of racially offensive material an arrestable offence (a serious offence for which a suspect can be arrested without a warrant).

The criminal law in Scotland provides similar protection against racial offences to that in England and Wales but relies on the common law rather than on statute.

Racial Harassment

The terms 'racial harassment' and 'racial attacks' cover a wide range of offences, from verbal abuse and graffiti to physical assault and arson. The Government is committed to combating racial harassment and has published two reports by an interdepartmental Racial Attacks Group, established in 1987 and chaired by the Home Office.

The first report, published in 1989, made recommendations for the police service, housing authorities and other organisations on combating racial attacks and harassment. Its main proposal was that local multi-agency groups should be set up to deal with racially motivated crime.

The second report, published in 1992, examined how far the Group's recommendations had been implemented. It acknowledged the involvement of many agencies in countering racial harassment, including the police service, local government authorities, the Crown Prosecution Service, the probation service, the CRE, racial equality councils, the Home Office's Safer Cities Programme[7], victim support schemes, and police and community consultative groups. It also identified the role of the courts in increasing public awareness, deterring potential offenders and raising the confidence of ethnic minority communities. The second report concluded that further co-ordinated action was still needed to implement fully the findings of the

[7] A crime prevention initiative launched in 1988 and now managed under the Single Regeneration Budget—see p. 31.

first report.

The Racial Attacks Group was reconvened by the Government in 1994 and is developing a wide-ranging programme including:

—the introduction of procedures to ensure that the racial motivation in a case is effectively highlighted;

—the exploration of the scope for prevention work; and

—the encouragement of more effective multi-agency work.

Similar initiatives and protections exist or are being developed in Scotland.

Under the Criminal Justice and Public Order Act 1994, anyone found guilty in England and Wales of the offence of causing intentional harassment, alarm or distress can be imprisoned for up to six months and/or fined up to £5,000. The new offence is being monitored to see how effective it is in dealing with racially motivated crime.

European Comparisons

Council of Europe
Britain has led other European countries in its approach to anti-discrimination and race relations, according to a report published by the Council of Europe on community and ethnic relations. The report, which was the result of an intergovernmental project carried out between 1987 and 1991, examined the approach to community relations by member states.

Britain, the report said, had gone further than other European countries in introducing anti-discrimination legislation and in setting up institutional provisions to promote racial equality. The report also recommended that other countries should follow Britain's example in:

—developing strategies for positive action (see p. 51);

—establishing genuine equal opportunities; and

—creating equal opportunities policies in police training and recruitment (see p. 78).

The CRE acts as the leading body for the British contribution to the Council of Europe's European youth campaign against racism and xenophobia. Called All Different All Equal, the campaign was agreed upon by 32 European states in 1993.

European Union

Another report, commissioned by the (then) Department of Employment in Britain and published in 1992, concluded that Britain had the most advanced law and practice on combating racial discrimination in employment in the European Union (EU).

According to the report:

—Britain had established a lead in good equal opportunities law and practice and was considerably ahead of its EU partners in dealing with indirect discrimination; and

—Britain was the only EU country where the vast majority of the ethnic minority communities enjoy voting rights.

Britain and its EU partners have issued a number of declarations denouncing manifestations of racism.

Government Programmes

Efforts have been made by successive governments and by local government authorities, increasingly in partnership with voluntary groups and private bodies, to tackle the problems of racial disadvantage. While the Home Secretary is the minister with general responsibility for race relations, each government department places great emphasis on the promotion of equality of opportunity and the elimination of racial disadvantage through its main expenditure programmes. The main sources of funds which channel extra resources to ethnic minorities are Home Office grants and the Single Regeneration Budget (SRB).

Home Office Grant

Under section 11 of the 1966 Local Government Act, the Government can pay grant to local authorities and certain education institutions, such as grant-maintained schools and further education colleges, to meet part of the cost of employing extra staff to help members of ethnic minorities to overcome language or cultural barriers. The grant provision in England and Wales in 1994–95 was about £50 million, covering some 4,000 posts. About 89 per cent of grant was allocated for education posts, mainly for providing teachers to teach English as a secondary language in schools. The remainder went to support posts in a number of other local authority service areas such as social services, employment, training and enterprise, and housing.

Since 1994–95, responsibility for some 55 per cent of

provision for section 11 grant has been transferred to the new SRB (see below). SRB has also taken in funds under the Ethnic Minority Grant which were paid by the Home Office through Training and Enterprise Councils (TECs—see p. 52) to support projects in England and Wales run by the voluntary sector. These projects aim to help members of ethnic minorities disadvantaged through differences of language and culture to gain employment, to enter vocational training, or to set up or improve their own businesses. At the beginning of 1994–95 the grant was supporting about 170 projects. Over £15 million has been spent on Ethnic Minority Grant projects since 1992–93.

In Scotland a new Ethnic Minority Grant scheme was introduced in 1992 to assist voluntary organisations with projects designed to promote racial equality and reduce racial disadvantage. The grant complements funding for urban regeneration projects in Scotland (the Urban Programme) and the support given to ethnic minority projects under existing Scottish social work legislation. Schemes awarded in 1995 include drug advice, information and advice for businesses, counselling services for women, and training of translators and interpreters.

Single Regeneration Budget

The SRB for England came into operation in 1994, bringing together and streamlining 20 programmes from five government departments (including City Challenge and Task Forces—see below) directed towards local regeneration. It is administered through Government Offices for the Regions and overseen by the Department of the Environment. The SRB's objectives are to:

—improve the employment prospects, education and skills of local people, particularly the young and those at a disadvantage, and promote equality of opportunity;

—encourage sustainable economic growth and wealth creation by improving the competitiveness of the local economy, including support for new and existing businesses;

—protect and improve the environment and infrastructure and promote good design;

—improve housing conditions for local people through physical improvements, better maintenance, improved management, greater choice and diversity;

—promote initiatives of benefit to ethnic minority communities;

—tackle crime and improve community safety; and

—enhance the quality of life of local people, including their health and their cultural and sports opportunities.

The SRB is providing £4,000 million over the three years 1996–97 to 1998–99. Of this over £1,300 million will be available for new projects from the SRB Challenge Fund. The balance of available SRB resources will continue to fund commitments on existing programmes, including Task Forces and City Challenge, which now form part of the SRB. Projects announced in December 1994 and December 1995 were intended to create or safeguard 500,000 jobs; support around 80,000 new businesses; complete or improve about 170,000 homes; and support some 20,000 voluntary and community groups. Over a third of these schemes are specifically directed towards ethnic minority communities.

City Challenge

The City Challenge initiative was launched in 1991 as a new approach to urban regeneration. Local authorities were invited to form partnerships with the public, private and voluntary sectors and local communities to identify the problems of run-down areas, develop solutions and bid for Department of the Environment funding of £37.5 million to implement five-year regeneration programmes. The needs of ethnic minority communities are addressed where appropriate. Examples of activity involving ethnic minorities from the first two rounds of City Challenge have included programmes in Bethnal Green and Blackburn.

Sixty per cent of the 14,000 people in the Bethnal Green City Challenge area are Black or Asian. For the Asian community the main problem is a lack of English language skills, a major barrier to employment. Bethnal Green's Language 2000 project is aiming to improve the language skills of the Asian residents. The project, which has now become a model in the provision of integrated language programmes, works in schools and also links language training for adults to customised training and access to higher education.

Half of the population of Blackburn's City Challenge area are from ethnic minority groups (predominantly Asian). Well over half of the housing is owner occupied, but 80 per cent is unfit or in disrepair. Local unemployment is over 26 per cent, which rises to more than 33 per cent for the ethnic minorities. A £73 million City Challenge multi-agency renewal programme is improving over 2,000 properties and building 300 new homes, some designed specifically for larger Asian families. Training programmes include management skills for ethnic minority businesses and computer and information technology skills for Asian women. Of the new jobs created and filled by City Challenge residents, half have been taken by people of Asian origin.

Task Forces

Locally-based inner city Task Forces, first set up in 1986, operate in some of the most deprived urban areas in England with populations of up to 60,000 people. They consist of small teams of civil servants, and secondees from local authorities and the private and voluntary sectors. Task Forces concentrate on the economic regeneration of designated inner city areas, by improving local people's employment prospects, by supporting training and education initiatives, and by identifying and removing barriers to their employment. They also aim to stimulate enterprise development and strengthen the capacity of communities to meet local needs. Forces are not intended to be permanent. Once a Task Force area has improved prospects for continued regeneration and local organisations have been strengthened, the Task Force is closed. There are currently eight Task Forces still open. Some of the projects supported by Task Forces have been tailored to meet the special needs of ethnic minorities.

Inner Cities Religious Council

The Inner Cities Religious Council, established in 1991, brings together regularly members from the Hindu, Jewish, Muslim, Sikh and Christian faiths, including the majority Black churches. The Council aims to provide the Government and religious groups with an effective way of working together for lasting improvements to the inner cities and deprived urban areas.

The Council is chaired by a government minister and

attended by members from all the five faiths. It is a forum for policy development and also provides a source of advice for faith communities on urban regeneration. A newsletter called *Faith Interaction* is published twice a year, and a programme of conferences is offered.

Advice and Research

An Advisory Council on Race Relations advises the Home Secretary on the development and implementation of race relations policies. It also provides a forum for ministers to discuss matters of concern with members of the ethnic minority communities and representatives of interested organisations. Within the Home Office there are two Community Relations Consultants providing specialist advice on race and community matters, including advice on the implementation of race relations policies for the police, probation, fire and prison services. The Department for Education and Employment has a Race Relations Employment Advisory Group, which advises ministers on issues relating to the employment of the ethnic minorities.

The need for factual information about questions concerning race relations on which to base policy decisions is reflected in the volume of research undertaken by government departments, official bodies including local authorities and racial equality councils, academic institutions and other independent organisations. The Home Office Research and Planning Unit undertakes studies to assist the department in its administrative functions. The Race Relations Employment Advisory Service in the Department for Education and Employment helps employers to develop and implement equal opportunities policies, including awareness training for senior managers and personnel staff, and the introduction of ethnic monitoring. Advisers are based in areas of high ethnic minority settlement.

Government departments also commission other official bodies and academic institutions to carry out research studies on their behalf. For example, a survey of Scotland's ethnic minority population was completed for The Scottish Office. Research is also supported by the Economic and Social Research Council, which funds the Centre for Research in Ethnic Relations based at Warwick University. The Commission for Racial Equality has published the results of many studies. Important enquiries are also carried out by the House of Commons Home Affairs Committee, most recently on racial attacks and harassment (see Further Reading).

Independent institutions which have published research studies on questions related to the position of ethnic minorities include the Policy Studies Institute, the National Foundation for Education Research, the Runnymede Trust, the Minority Rights Group, the Refugee Council and the Joint Council for Welfare of Immigrants.

The Council of Churches for Britain and Ireland has a long-established Churches' Commission for Racial Justice. The Society of Friends addresses racial issues through its Community Relations Committee. The Catholic Association for Racial Justice has a publications programme in progress. A major Church of England report on the problems of the inner cities and other areas of social deprivation, entitled *Faith in the City*, was published in 1985. A second report, *Living Faith in the City*, was published in 1990, and a third report, called *Staying in the City*, in November 1995. The Muslim community held their first Community Development Conference in 1996.

Employment

Policies to enable the ethnic minorities to compete for work on more equal terms have been formulated by the Department for Education and Employment. These efforts to alleviate disadvantage and discrimination are supported by trade unions, many large employers and the CRE. The Department aims to increase employers' awareness and understanding of the race relations legislation and to encourage them to provide equal opportunities for all people regardless of ethnic origin.

Employment Patterns and Status

Data from the *Labour Force Survey* in spring 1994 indicated that some 5.9 per cent of the population of working age (16 to 64 for men and 16 to 59 for women) in Great Britain, or nearly 2 million people, were from ethnic minority groups (see Table 5). Of these, 560,000 were of Indian ethnic origin, 530,000 were Black and 440,000 were of Pakistani or Bangladeshi origin; the remainder were mainly Chinese, mixed or of other origins.

Table 6 details the economic activity rate of people of working age by ethnic group and sex. Overall, 77 per cent of ethnic minority men and 52 per cent of women in Great Britain were economically active, compared with 86 per cent of men and 72 per cent of women in the White population. The economic activity rates within the ethnic minorities were highest in the Black (73 per cent) and Indian (71 per cent) groups, compared with 79 per cent for the White group. The economic activity rate for the

Table 5: Ethnic Minority Groups of Working Age as a Percentage of Each Age Group, Great Britain, Spring 1994[a]

Age group	All	Men	Women
16–24	7.4	7.1	7.7
25–34	7.0	6.4	7.7
35–44	6.1	6.0	6.3
45–59/64	3.8	3.9	3.7
All	5.9	5.6	6.2

Source: Labour Force Survey

[a] Table not seasonally adjusted.

Pakistani and Bangladeshi group was 49 per cent. The rates among women of working age were considerably higher in the Black (67 per cent) and Indian (62 per cent) groups than in the Pakistani and Bangladeshi groups (26 per cent), possibly due partly to different cultural attitudes towards marriage and towards women having jobs.

Economic activity rates among young people in the 16 to 24 age range were lower in the ethnic minority groups (48 per cent overall) than in the White population (72 per cent). This was due in part to the higher proportion of ethnic minority young people staying in full-time education (48 per cent) than White young people (31 per cent). It may also reflect greater difficulty in obtaining employment: at every level of qualification held, ethnic minorities are twice as likely to be unemployed as White people with the same qualification.

Table 6: Economic Activity Rates by Age Group and
Ethnic Origin, Great Britain, Spring 1994   *Percentage*

Age/Ethnic origin	All	Men	Women
16–59/64			
All origins[a]	78	85	71
White	79	86	72
Non-White	64	77	52
Black	73	79	67
Indian	71	80	62
Pakistani/Bangladeshi	49	75	26
Mixed/Other	61	72	51
16–24			
All origins[a]	70	75	65
White	72	77	67
Non-White	48	54	42
Black	56	62	51
Indian	53	55	51
Pakistani/Bangladeshi	45	57	35
Mixed/Other	40	45	34
25–34			
All origins[a]	83	95	71
White	84	95	72
Non-White	70	86	56
Black	76	84	69
Indian	78	93	67
Pakistani/Bangladeshi	57	97	25
Mixed/Other	63	75	52

continued

Table 6 continued

35–44			
All origins[a]	85	94	77
White	86	94	78
Non-White	75	90	60
Black	81	89	73
Indian	83	93	71
Pakistani/Bangladeshi	54	87	23
Mixed/Other	75	90	63
45–59/64			
All origins[a]	75	79	70
White	75	79	70
Non-White	64	75	51
Black	75	77	72
Indian	66	76	53
Pakistani/Bangladeshi	41	63	[b]
Mixed/Other	68	80	54

Source: Labour Force Survey
[a] Includes those who did not indicate their ethnic origin.
[b] Less than 10,000 in cell; estimate not shown.

Types of Work

Since the mid-1980s there has been a growth in non-manual occupations for both White and ethnic minority men and women, so that in 1993 roughly the same proportion of both groups held non-manual jobs (about 60 per cent).

For male employees, the overall proportion of ethnic minority workers in non-manual occupations (51 per cent) was slightly lower than for White males (53 per cent). However, there were larger variations among the different ethnic minority groups (as shown in Table 7); 53 per cent of Indian employees were in non-manual occupations, compared with 41 per cent of Pakistanis and Bangladeshis and 45 per cent of Black employees. Among employed women, the proportion in non-manual occupations was around two-thirds for almost all ethnic groups, except for the Indian group, where the proportion between non-manual and manual was 61 per cent and 39 per cent respectively.

Table 7: Manual and Non-Manual Employment by Ethnic Group, Great Britain, Spring 1994 *Percentage*

Ethnic origin	All employ-ees[a]	All Non-manual[b]	Manual	Men Non-manual	Manual	Women Non-manual	Manual
All origins[c]	21,273	61	38	53	46	70	30
White	20,427	61	38	53	46	70	30
Ethnic minority groups	840	58	41	51	49	67	33
Black	265	56	43	45	53	66	33
Indian	269	57	43	53	46	61	39
Pakistani/ Bangla-deshi	114	51	49	41	59	73	27
Mixed/ Other	192	68	32	62	38	73	26

Source: Labour Force Survey

[a] Thousands = 100 per cent.
[b] Includes those who did not state whether they were in manual or non-manual employment or those serving in the armed forces.
[c] Includes those who did not state origin.

Table 8 shows that White people were more likely to work for the private sector (62 per cent) than those from ethnic minorities (57 per cent). This pattern was more marked for women (60 per cent of White women work in the private sector compared with 54 per cent of ethnic minority women) than for men (63 per cent White and 59 per cent non-white). This difference was mostly accounted for by Black women being more likely to work in the public sector (51 per cent compared with 31 per cent for all women). For men, the difference was due to higher self-employment among the Asian group (23 per cent of Indian men and 26 per cent of Pakistani and Bangladeshi men compared with 17 per cent of White men), although Black men were less likely to be self-employed (10 per cent) and more likely to be working in the public sector (32 per cent).

In spring 1994 more White women in employment were working part-time than women from the ethnic minorities (46 per cent and 33 per cent respectively). However, for the relatively small group of Pakistani and Bangladeshi women who were working, the part-time proportion was similar to that for White women (43 per cent). Men from the ethnic minorities were more likely than their White counterparts to work part-time (10 per cent compared with 7 per cent). The highest proportion (14 per cent) again occurred in the Pakistani and Bangladeshi group. Further details are shown in Table 9.

Table 8: People in Employment by Sex, Ethnic Origin and Employment Status, Great Britain, Spring 1994

Percentage

Sex Employment status	All origins[a]	White	All	Black	Indian	Pakistani/ Bangladeshi	Mixed/ other
			Ethnic minority groups				
All							
All in employment[b]	24,942	23,909	1,025	294	343	156	233
All employees[c]	85	85	82	90	79	73	82
Private sector	61	62	57	49	60	61	60
Public sector	24	24	25	41	19	12	23
Self-employed	13	13	15	7	18	22	14
Men							
All in employment[b]	13,716	13,139	574	146	190	110	128
All employees[c]	81	81	77	87	74	71	77
Private sector	63	63	59	55	58	65	60
Public sector	18	18	18	32	16	[d]	17
Self-employed	17	17	20	10	23	26	19
Women							
All in employment[b]	11,226	10,770	451	148	153	46	105
All employees[c]	91	91	88	94	84	79	89
Private sector	59	60	54	43	62	53	59
Public sector	31	31	34	51	22	26	30
Self-employed	7	7	8	[d]	11	[d]	[d]

Source: Labour Force Survey

[a] Includes those who did not state origin.

[b] Includes those in government training and employment schemes; '000 = 100%.

[c] Includes those who did not state whether they worked in the public or private sector.

[d] Less than 10,000 in cell; estimate not shown.

Table 9: People in Part-time Employment by Sex and Ethnic Origin, Spring 1994[a] *Percentage*

Sex	All origins	White	Ethnic minority groups				
			All	Black	Indian	Pakistani/ Bangladeshi	Mixed/ other
All	25	26	21	22	18	23	22
Male	7	7	10	9	7	14	12
Female	46	46	33	33	31	43	32

Source: Labour Force Survey

[a] Table not seasonally adjusted.

Unemployment

According to the *Labour Force Survey* for spring 1994, unemployment rates for ethnic minority groups were higher than those for the White population (21 per cent compared with 9 per cent), although there were wide variations among the different ethnic groups. The highest unemployment rates were among the Black and Pakistani/Bangladeshi communities (26 and 28 per cent respectively). Among the 16–24 age group more than half of all Black Caribbean men were unemployed, compared with 18 per cent of White men. In the next age group (25–34), Indians were not much more likely to be unemployed than their White counterparts (11 per cent compared with 9 per cent). Unemployment rates in other ethnic minority groups, however, were double those for White people.

Table 10: Unemployment Rates by Ethnic Origin, Great Britain, Spring 1994 *Percentage*

Ethnic origin	All	Men	Women
All origins[a]	10	11	7
White	9	11	7
Non-White	21	25	16
Black	26	33	17
Indian	14	16	12
Pakistani/ Bangladeshi	28	29	24
Mixed/Other	19	22	16

Source: Labour Force Survey

[a] Includes those who did not indicate their ethnic origin.

Employment by Sector and Occupation

The majority of both the White and ethnic minority populations work in the service sector. Those least likely to work in service industries are White and Black Caribbean men and women, and men from the South Asian groups. This is largely due to higher proportions of these groups working in manufacturing. Overall there is a greater than average concentration of Black men and women in the public sector, while Indian, Pakistani and Bangladeshi men and women are more likely than average to be self-employed.

Since the mid-1980s employment in the manufacturing industries has declined by around 9 per cent for the White population but by twice as much for the ethnic minority groups. At the same time, employment in the service sector has grown by nearly 50 per cent for ethnic minorities compared with 15 per cent for White people.

Within these broad categories, there is a noticeable concentration in particular industries (see Figure 2). Women are concentrated in a narrower range of industries than men, as are ethnic minority groups compared with the White population. About a fifth of women from each ethnic minority group work in a single industry. Gender differences persist across different ethnic groups, with women being more likely than men to work in retail distribution and in medical services. However, among ethnic minority groups the gender differences are far less distinct than in the White population. For example, South Asian men are also highly concentrated in retail distribution, and there are high concentrations of Chinese men and women in the restaurant sector. In 1991 there were five times more South Asian women working in the manufacture of footwear and clothing than any other ethnic group (including White). Black and White men were far more likely to work in the construction industry than men in any other ethnic groups.

Women from all ethnic groups, including White, are concentrated in a small number of occupations compared with most groups of men. Women are particularly likely to work in clerical or secretarial occupations, personal services or as health associate professionals, whereas higher proportions of men work as managers or in skilled trades. According to the 1991 Census, about 5 per cent of ethnic minority women and 7 per cent of ethnic minority men worked as managers and administrators, compared with 12 per cent of White men and 6 per cent of White women.

Ethnic minority groups, especially the Chinese population, overall work longer hours than the White population. According to the *Labour Force Survey* for spring 1994, average hourly earnings of ethnic minority employees working full-time were about 92 per cent of those of White employees. Women from ethnic minorities earned roughly the same per hour as White women, while ethnic minority men earned 89 per cent of White men's earnings.

In London almost 19 per cent of the economically active population of working age were from the ethnic minorities and 40 per cent of these were Black.

Action to Remove Disadvantage

People from ethnic minority groups tend to be concentrated in lower skilled jobs. Research has shown that discrimination, though not always conscious or intentional, affects both recruitment and promotion prospects of members of ethnic minority groups. A major way in which the Government seeks to combat these disadvantages is by encouraging employers to promote racial equality of opportunity in employment.

Figure 2: Ethnic Minority Employment by Industrial Sector

Proportion of female employment by industrial sector
Three largest sectors for each ethnic group

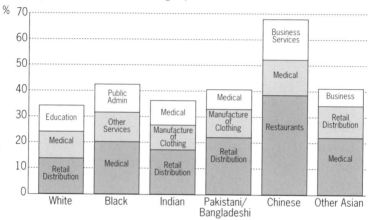

Proportion of male employment by industrial sector
Three largest sectors for each ethnic group

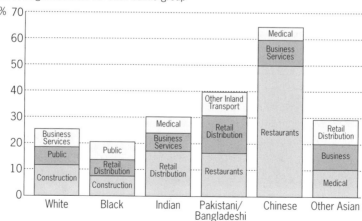

Source: *Black and Ethnic Minority Women and Men*
Equal Opportunities Commission.

Code of Practice

The CRE's 1984 code of practice recommends that employers should ensure that:

—a job applicant or employee does not receive less favourable treatment than another on racial grounds;

—an applicant or employee is not placed at a disadvantage by requirements or conditions which have a disproportionate effect on his or her racial group and which cannot be shown to be justifiable on other grounds; and

—where appropriate and legally permissible, employees of under-represented racial groups should be given training and encouragement to achieve equal opportunity within the organisation.

Employers Standard for Equality

In January 1995 the CRE published a practical guide, *Racial Equality Means Business*, an employer standard for equality which aims to help employers assess what has been done to combat racial discrimination at the work place and what action is needed to make a real impact in removing discrimination. Employers are encouraged to take specific steps, including encouraging applicants from particular groups in which they are under-represented, for example through outreach to community groups. The guide also suggests establishing support groups, mentoring schemes and shadowing existing staff. In areas of skill shortages, employers could sponsor scholarships and give bursaries that would provide training and work experience.

Ten-Point Plan for Employers

An Equal Opportunities Ten-Point Plan for Employers, published by the (then) Department of Employment, gives practical advice on how employers can offer equality of opportunity for their employees and job applicants regardless of their race, gender or any disability. The Plan advises employers to:

—develop an equal opportunities policy including recruitment, promotion and training;

—set an action plan including targets;

— provide equal opportunities training for all;

—monitor the present position and progress in achieving objectives;

—review recruitment, selection, promotion and training procedures regularly;

—draw up clear and justifiable job criteria;

—offer pre-employment training and positive action training;

—consider their image among potential employees;

—consider flexible working arrangements; and

—develop links with local community groups, organisations and schools.

The Plan states that discrimination in employment 'is not only morally wrong, it is bad for business and may be unlawful'. It maintains that equality of opportunity can reduce recruitment and training costs, raise morale and improve customer relations. It also says that providing equality of opportunity is a natural and integral part of good management practice.

Equal Opportunities in the Civil Service

The Government is committed to providing equality of opportunity for all its staff. In support of this commitment, the Civil Service, which recruits and promotes on the basis of merit, is actively pursuing policies to develop career opportunities for women,[8] people of ethnic minority origin and people with disabilities. The Civil Service Data Summary 1994, published by the Cabinet Office, revealed that ethnic minority representation across the Civil Service increased from 4.2 per cent in 1989 to 5.3 per cent in 1994. This compared favourably with 4.8 per cent in the economically active population and should be viewed against a background of reducing Civil Service numbers overall.

People of ethnic minority origin are highly represented in junior grade levels, with lower (but slowly increasing) representation at more senior levels. This partly reflects differences in the age and length of service of different racial groups.

All departments and agencies include equal opportunities in recruitment, promotion, appraisal and management training courses.

Positive Action

The Race Relations Act 1976 contains provisions for allowing positive action in certain circumstances (see p. 20). Under the Act employers and other bodies may give encouragement and training to people from a particular racial group to help them gain access to particular work in which members of that group have been under-represented. Employers may also offer training to employees from a particular racial group to fit them for particular work in which members of that group have been

[8]For further information see *Women* (Aspects of Britain: HMSO, 1996).

under-represented, or may encourage people from that racial group to take advantage of opportunities for doing that work. However, in all cases selection for jobs must be on merit.

Positive action gives considerable scope for opening up job opportunities and improving career development for ethnic minority employees. Employers benefit by reaching a wider labour market and realising under-used potential.

Training

The Department for Education and Employment is responsible for overseeing government-funded training programmes for adults and young people, to which members of ethnic minority groups have equal access. In Scotland responsibility lies with the Scottish Education and Industry Department.

In England and Wales a network of employer-led TECs plan and develop the quality, effectiveness and relevance of training and enterprise at local level. In Scotland, Local Enterprise Companies (LECs) provide a similar service.

TECs and LECs have a contractual responsibility to ensure equality of opportunity. Guidance has been produced for staff and training providers on how to develop and implement an effective equal opportunities strategy. Where there is a significant ethnic minority community in a TEC area, the Department for Education and Employment expects to see the interests of that community represented on the board and involved in advisory groups. TECs are also expected to consult local communities whilst drawing up their business and corporate plans.

TECs and LECs manage the Training for Work programme, which aims to help long-term unemployed people find jobs and to improve their work-related skills. Those people with little English language or low levels of literacy skills are eligible to join the programme without having to be unemployed for six months.

Another scheme managed by the TECs and LECs is Youth Training, which provides broad-based vocational education and quality training to give young people the modern skills and qualifications they require to get worthwhile jobs. Other schemes include:

—Youth Credits, run in Scotland under the Skillseekers scheme, which offer young people who have left full-time education an entitlement to join the labour market to train to approved standards. Credits can be presented to an employer or training provider in exchange for training; and

—Modern Apprenticeships, which are designed to increase the number of young people trained to technician, supervisory and equivalent levels. An accelerated version of this scheme provides high-level training for those aged 18 and 19.

Ethnic Minority Business Initiative
The Ethnic Minority Business Initiative was established by the Government in 1985 to encourage the development of ethnic minority businesses and enterprise. Five Black-led local enterprise agencies were set up in Deptford, Finsbury Park and Wandsworth in London, Handsworth in Birmingham, and in Bristol. Initially, these focused on the Black Caribbean community, but the scope of the scheme has since been widened to include other disadvantaged groups through support for more enterprise agencies. In 1995–96 the initiative funded 13 organ-

isations which provide a range of advice directed at both new and existing businesses.

The Ethnic Minority Business Initiative is administered by the Department of the Environment as part of the SRB (see p. 31).

Trade Unions

The Trades Union Congress (TUC) and many individual unions have taken steps to put equal opportunities policies into practice. The TUC has published a Charter for Black Workers and has produced multilingual trade union literature. A new section for Black women has been established on the TUC's general council. The CRE assisted the TUC's Equal Rights Unit in drawing up a lay adviser's manual and is contributing legal specialists to a training programme in racial discrimination cases for trade union officials.

In 1994 a slightly lower proportion of ethnic minority employees than their White counterparts (29 per cent as opposed to 32 per cent) were members of trade unions. Ethnic minorities accounted for about 4 per cent of trade union membership in 1994.

Education

Most children from the ethnic minorities now starting school were born in Britain and tend to share the interests and aspirations of other children in their schools. Nevertheless, many of them still experience difficulties arising from cultural differences, including those of language, religion and customs. In addition, the concentration of some ethnic minority communities in the inner city areas where social and economic deprivation are most severe has meant that many of them share with others the educational disadvantage associated with such areas.

Government Policies

The Government has endorsed a code of practice for the elimination of racial discrimination in education, published by the CRE in 1989. The code outlines the application of the Race Relations Act to education, and identifies practices which may constitute unlawful racial discrimination. It applies in England and Wales; a Scottish code was published in 1991.

In 1985 the Committee of Inquiry into the Education of Children from Ethnic Minority Groups, under the chairmanship of the late Lord Swann, published a major report, *Education for All* (see Further Reading). This heralded government action to reduce underachievement among some ethnic minority pupils and to improve the responsiveness of the education service to ethnic diversity. Initiatives included action on initial and in-service teacher training; measures to increase recruitment of ethnic minority teachers; funding for pilot projects directed at meeting educational needs in a multi-ethnic society, including some designed specifically to promote good race relations; and action on the curriculum and examinations.

Various schools inspectorates report to the Government on educational standards. Commitment to equal opportunities form an essential element of such inspections.[9]

Schools

The Government believes that ethnic minority groups should be equipped with the knowledge, skills and understanding to participate on equal terms in all aspects of British life, while remaining free to maintain their own cultural identity.

In the case of children whose parents do not speak English at home, a first priority is to acquire a fluent command of English. Local education authorities and schools have made extensive provision for English language support to meet this need. Provision is also increasingly being made for the support of mother-tongue teaching in schools, especially in the early primary years, as a means of ensuring access to the curriculum and facilitating the acquisition of English. Schools have also to take account of the ethnic and cultural background of pupils, and curricula should reflect ethnic and cultural diversity.

A survey report published in 1994 by OFSTED (the independent Office for Standards in Education) found that standards of education achieved by pupils from ethnic minority backgrounds had improved with the help of funding under section 11 of the 1966 Local Government Act (see p. 30).

see p. 30

[9]For further information see *Education* (Aspects of Britain: HMSO, 1996).

Ethnic Monitoring

The Government has acknowledged the need to collect statistics on the ethnic origins, languages and religions of schoolchildren to ensure that education meets the needs of all pupils, thereby helping to secure equality of opportunity. In 1990 maintained schools began collecting ethnically based information provided voluntarily by parents, covering pupils aged 5 to 11. Returns are submitted to the Government every year.

In Scotland similar information is provided annually by schools at certain stages in both primary and secondary education.

National Curriculum

A broad and balanced National Curriculum for children aged 5 to 16 has been introduced in all state schools in England and Wales. It consists of the core subjects of English, mathematics and science, and a number of other subjects. National criteria for the General Certificate of Secondary Education (GCSE—the main examination for testing National Curriculum subjects at the age of 16) require that syllabuses and examinations should be free of ethnic bias.

In Scotland there is no National Curriculum and the responsibility for the delivery of the curriculum rests with education authorities and school managers, under guidance issued by The Scottish Office Education Department. There is equal opportunity in terms of access to the curriculum regardless of race, sex, religion and social factors.

Bodies responsible for the National Curriculum and its assessment arrangements in England and Wales are required to take account of the ethnic and cultural diversity of British society and of the importance of promoting equal opportunities for all pupils. The Scottish Examination Board applies similar criteria.

A modern foreign language is a National Curriculum foundation subject at secondary level. A choice of languages includes the working languages of the EU, together with Arabic, Bengali, Gujarati, Hindi, Japanese, Mandarin or Cantonese Chinese, Modern Hebrew, Punjabi, Russian, Turkish and Urdu. All schools must offer at least one working EU language and may in addition offer one of the other listed languages.

In Scotland it is recommended that a modern European language should be learned by all pupils throughout the first four years of compulsory education, although a second language may also be offered.

Religious Education

Religious education is taught by all schools. Their syllabuses must reflect the fact that the religious traditions in Britain are mainly Christian, while taking account of the teaching and practices of the other principal religions represented. The precise balance between Christianity and other religions is decided locally. Schools in England, Northern Ireland and Wales are also required to provide a daily act of worship. This must be of a broadly Christian character, though there is flexibility for this requirement to be lifted if the head teacher considers it inappropriate for some or all pupils.

In Scotland guidance has been issued to education authorities recommending that religious education and observance in schools should be similarly based on Christianity while promoting understanding of, and respect for, those who adhere to different faiths.

Parents are entitled to withdraw their children from religious education classes and acts of collective worship.

Parental Choice

The Government attaches great importance to meeting parents' wishes about the education of their children. A number of measures have been taken in the last ten years to widen the choice of schools available and to increase parental involvement in school organisation.

Parents have a statutory right to express a preference for the school they would like their children to attend and local education authorities have a general duty to meet parents' wishes. In order to increase parental choice, legislation requires schools to admit pupils up to their standard number. They cannot refuse admission to any child unless that number has been reached. The standard number is an indicator of the size of the school. These measures have given help for Muslim families, in particular, seeking admission to a single-sex school and make it easier for families living in areas where there are no such schools to apply to schools in neighbouring authorities' areas.

Questions have arisen in some areas over the dress of Muslim girls, sex education and the availability of 'Halal' meat (meat from an animal slaughtered according to Islamic law). These matters have been the subject of local discussion and in some cases, notably in Bradford, special arrangements have been made.

Liaison between the school and the home is considered important and many authorities with significant ethnic minority populations have made particular efforts to forge such links. Parents from ethnic minorities are encouraged to stand for election to the governing bodies of their children's schools.

Teachers

Teacher-training institutions are encouraged to ensure that students are adequately prepared for teaching in a multi-ethnic society. Initial training courses offer relevant studies, including subsidiary studies in teaching English as a second language. Special courses to enable students from ethnic minorities to reach the standard necessary for entry into teaching have helped recruitment. The Government has also attempted to attract more ethnic minority members into the profession through advertising and publicity campaigns and exhibitions. Initial teacher training courses have been developed which draw on the linguistic and other skills, experience and qualifications of mature ethnic minority students.

Post-school Education

Post-school education for young people is provided at a range of levels in universities and colleges of higher and further education. A major part of the provision is for vocational education, including courses leading to recognised qualifications, and training for people in employment.

According to the spring 1994 *Labour Force Survey*, a much greater proportion of young ethnic minority people were in full-time education than White (48 per cent compared with 31 per cent). In general, the percentage of men and women from the ethnic minorities in full-time education was more than twice the rate for White men and women. The only exception was Pakistani/Bangladeshi young women (28 per cent compared with 31 per cent of young White women), who also have a low economic activity rate (see Table 6, p. 39). While participation in full-time education was similar for White men and women in the 16-24 age group (31 per cent), more young Black women than men (52 per cent compared with 36 per cent) were full-time students. However, in other ethnic groups more young men than women were in education.

Further education colleges play an important part in the schemes administered by the TECs for unemployed people (see p. 52), including basic courses in literacy and numeracy. In addition, many colleges offer courses designed to provide entry to universities and colleges of higher education, as well as courses in English as a second language and remedial English.

The ethnic monitoring of students enrolling on further and higher education courses has been introduced.

The National Equal Opportunities Higher Education Network brings together academic and administrative staff concerned with equal opportunity in areas such as student access, curriculum development and employment.

Further Education for Adults

The teaching of English for adults whose native tongue is not English (English for Speakers of Other Languages—ESOL) is given a high priority. The Further Education Funding Council in England and Wales has a statutory responsibility to attract more people into further education from traditionally underrepresented sections of the community, including adults from ethnic minorities.

Access courses provide an alternative route to higher education for mature students without traditional entry requirements. They are designed to meet the needs of identified groups in the community, including ethnic minority adults, who may be under-represented in higher education.

The Youth Service

The Youth Service—a partnership between local government and voluntary organisations—is concerned with the informal personal and social education of young people aged 11 to 25 (5 to 25 in Northern Ireland). Work with young people from the ethnic minorities is one of the priorities for the Youth Service, which can help counter prejudice and discrimination. The Department for Education and Employment's scheme of grants to National Voluntary Youth Organisations includes funding for programmes to help meet the needs of young members of ethnic minority communities.

Social Welfare

Health and personal social services, provided largely free of charge, are available to everyone normally resident in Britain.[10] The various statutory and voluntary bodies concerned aim to deal with any special difficulties experienced by the ethnic minority communities and a number of initiatives directed at specific groups have been undertaken. The social security system provides benefits for people who are elderly, sick, disabled, unemployed, widowed or bringing up children, together with certain income-related benefits for those without adequate means of support.

Health Services

The Government is fully committed to eliminating racial discrimination in the National Health Service (NHS) and to promoting equality of opportunity in health service delivery. The Government's Patient's Charter states that the NHS has a duty to ensure that its users are treated fairly, by respecting their privacy, dignity, and religious and cultural beliefs. Since 1989 the Department of Health has funded projects to improve information for ethnic minorities and access to services. A number of White and ethnic minority organisations have been funded to produce access information materials such as videos and leaflets and also to work with local groups.

[10]For further information see *Social Welfare* (Aspects of Britain: HMSO, 1995).

A number of initiatives have been undertaken to improve health care for ethnic minority communities, for example:

—popular versions of the Government's 1992 White Paper *The Health of the Nation*, which sets out a strategy for improving the nation's health, have been translated in 11 minority languages;

—a guide entitled *Ethnicity and Health: A Guide for the NHS* was published in 1993, covering areas of general health concern such as cancer and heart disease, as well as key areas specific to people of different ethnic origins, such as thalassaemia and sickle cell disorder (see p. 66);

—a publication produced jointly by the Department of Health and the Royal College of Physicians of London entitled *Access to Health Care for People from Black and Ethnic Minorities*, which examines problems of access and proposes solutions for purchasers of health care to improve the health services for ethnic minority people;

—an information exchange on ethnic minority health, funded by the Department of Health and run by the King's Fund (an independent charity), which gathers and disseminates information about individuals and organisations working to improve health services for ethnic minorities, and holds relevant demographic and epidemiological data; and

—a Department of Health-funded booklet, *Checklist on Health and Race*, to enable NHS managers to make the service more appropriate and accessible.

Improving access to health services for ethnic minorities is a priority. To build upon the examples of good practice that have been developed throughout the NHS, the Department of Health funded the production of a practical guide for health purchasers and providers to assess how far they have progressed in ensuring that their provision of services is sensitive to the cultural and religious needs of different ethnic minority communities.

To improve information about the use of health services by people from ethnic minorities, it is now mandatory to record the ethnic origin of patients who use in-patient or day-care services. Such data enables purchasers and providers to examine the up-take of services, monitor standards and identify any gaps in service provision.

Another government project is the Ethnic Health Unit, set up in 1993 to encourage initiatives in England which would improve the responsiveness of the NHS to the needs of people from ethnic minorities. A key element of the Unit's work is organising the funding of projects designed by health authorities, hospital and community trusts in partnership with local ethnic minority organisations. Current initiatives managed by the Unit include:

—a maternity link project for Vietnamese women;

—a project to improve communication and consultation between elderly Black people and their local health authority;

—a primary care scheme to improve access to screening, prevention and treatment services for ethnic minority women and children; and

—the promotion among South Asian communities of prevention and treatment services for coronary heart disease and diabetes.

The Health Education Board for Scotland is funding a collaborative project with the Health Promotion Department of Greater Glasgow Health Board which is looking into the health information needs of ethnic minority communities, particularly women in relation to breast and cervical cancer and diabetes. The project will be completed by March 1997.

Provision of Care

Health education is a major factor in safeguarding the health of the ethnic minorities. Family doctors, child health clinics and health visitors to the home are all involved in this aspect of health care. The staff of the maternity and child health clinics look after the health of pregnant women and children up to school age. After children start school they are the concern of the school health service and the family doctor.

Link workers, who are fluent in English and at least one ethnic minority language, are employed within the NHS to help overcome barriers of language and culture between patients and health professionals.

The incidence of certain diseases is higher among some ethnic minority groups than in the overall population. Special measures are being taken to eradicate these diseases. For example, mortality from coronary heart disease has been shown to be higher in these groups than the national average and the Department of Health has produced a video advising ethnic minority communities of the risks of the disease.

A small but significant number of people in certain ethnic minority groups carry life-threatening genetic disorders such as sickle cell anaemia and thalassaemia. The Department of Health contributes funds to the Sickle Cell Society and the UK

Thalassaemia Society to help provide information and education material for sufferers and families, the health care profession and the wider public. It has helped finance the production of a video aimed at teaching children about sickle cell disease, and one on thalassaemia featuring an Asian family and dubbed in various Asian languages.

An information pack on the mental health needs of the Asian community provides guidance for mental health professionals on cultural, linguistic and religious issues. The Department has also funded the production of a multicultural video and support material on psychiatric care for ethnic minorities, and of a multicultural video and supporting leaflets on psychotherapy in a range of Asian languages.

Codes of Practice

The CRE's Code of Practice in Primary Health Care Services was launched in 1992. Endorsed by the Government, it applies to primary health services in England, Scotland and Wales. The code provides:

—guidance on the operation of the Race Relations Act 1976 and the elimination of racial discrimination in employment and service provision; and

—examples of good practice in the implementation and promotion of equal opportunities.

The code states that the basic components of a race equality policy are:

—commitment to the elimination of discrimination in primary health care services and to the provision of adequate services accessible to all sections of the community;

—ethnic monitoring of service users and regular reviews of policies and procedures; and

—a declaration that the service provider will abide by the race relations legislation and the code.

The code recognises that race equality training is vital for the effective implementation of non-discriminatory practices and procedures. It also emphasises that primary health service providers should consider translating all relevant information into the various languages used in their area and providing interpreting services wherever necessary.

The CRE also issued a race relations code of practice in the maternity services in 1994.

Personal Social Services

Local authority social services departments, and social work departments in Scotland, provide or arrange for the provision of personal social services for people with social care needs. These focus on the care and protection of children, on families experiencing problems, on people with physical or learning disability, people who are mentally ill, older people and people with alcohol and drug problems. In Scotland, local authorities are responsible for social work services in the criminal justice system. They also provide and support services for the victims of crime, including those from ethnic minorities.

There are vulnerable members of society among the ethnic minority groups just as there are in the rest of the population, but problems experienced by ethnic minorities may be compounded by differences of language, social attitudes and religion. Although ethnic minority members are well represented in certain sections of the personal social services—for example, working in the home help service and in residential homes for children and adults, particularly the elderly—they have been under-represented in field social work. However, the recruitment of social workers from the ethnic minorities is encouraged.

The Department of Health funds the Race Equality Unit, which offers a consultancy service to local authority social services departments on good practice in the delivery of services to ethnic minorities. Also, an increasing number of local authorities have created specialist posts for race advisers or development officers.

Child Care

Local authorities have a duty to register day nurseries, playgroups and childminders, and to ensure that day care services for young children meet acceptable standards. They also have to review the day care services in their area and publish a report.

Legislation requires local authorities, in making their arrangements for day care, to 'have regard to the different racial groups to which children within their area who are in need belong'. Local authorities should:

—have approved equal opportunities policies, including arrangements for monitoring and reviewing progress towards implementation;

—ensure that they have available data on the ethnic origins of the local population in order to assess the extent to which day care and educational services for the under-fives are operating in a non-discriminatory way; and

—involve all racial groups in the exercise of the review duty.

The Government believes that ethnic minority children who need substitute families should have the opportunity of placement with families which share their ethnic origin and religion. Under the Children Act 1989, where local authorities look after children, they have a duty to give due consideration to the child's religious persuasion, racial origin, and cultural and linguistic background. Also, where the courts are considering making an order under the Act, they are required in most situations to have regard to the child's background and characteristics, including race and culture.

Voluntary societies have traditionally played an important part in the provision of personal social services, and ethnic minority groups have themselves started a large number of organisations. In England and Wales, the National Federation of Self-Help Organisations acts as a co-ordinating body for such groups.

Social Security

The Department of Social Security produces information about social security benefits, including a leaflet entitled *Which Benefit?* in 11 languages other than English (Arabic, Bengali, Chinese, Greek, Gujarati, Hindi, Punjabi, Somali, Turkish, Urdu, and Vietnamese). There is also a free telephone advice and information service in Urdu, Punjabi and Chinese.

All Benefits Agency offices are required to make arrangements for interpreting when it is necessary to interview a customer who does not speak English. Training courses for local social office staff help to equip them to serve a multiracial community.

Efforts have been made to achieve common standards of equality of service delivery and the implementation of good anti-discriminatory practice in local benefit offices. The commitment of the Department of Social Security to racial equality has been re-emphasised by the Benefits Agency's Customer Charter, which aims to provide 'helpful and accessible assistance and information' while recognising the particular needs of people from ethnic minorities.

Housing

Evidence suggests that the housing conditions of ethnic minorities have improved significantly since their initial settlement in Britain although, overall, substantial inequalities between White and Black remain.

Types of Tenure

1991 Census figures for England, Scotland and Wales indicated considerable differences in the type of housing occupied by ethnic minority groups, and between each group and the White population.

Among the Asian population, 82 per cent of Indians, 77 per cent of Pakistanis, 62 per cent of Chinese and 44.5 per cent of Bangladeshis owned or were buying their house or flat. This compared with 67 per cent of the White population. Of the Black ethnic groups, Black Caribbeans had the highest rate of owner-occupancy at 48 per cent. Overall, some 13 per cent of the ethnic minority groups lived in privately-rented accommodation.

Among Black groups, between 34 and 41 per cent rented housing from local authorities, and between 9 and 11 per cent from housing associations. With the exception of the Bangladeshi group, a much lower proportion of the Asian population lived in these types of accommodation. About 21 per cent of the White population rented local authority housing.

In Scotland, the Asian community, although small, was found mainly in owner-occupied flats in the principal cities.

Local Authority Rented Homes

Most of the public housing in Britain is provided by local government authorities and the rest by many housing associations (see below). Tenants of public housing in England, Scotland and Wales have statutory rights which include security of tenure. Most tenants of local authority housing have the right to buy their accommodation, often at substantial discounts.

Housing Associations

Non-profit-making housing associations provide accommodation for rent or sale through new building or the rehabilitation of older property. With government encouragement housing associations have grown in importance.

Housing schemes carried out by associations registered with the Housing Corporation in England, Scottish Homes or Tai Cymru in Wales qualify for government grant. These three statutory bodies promote, supervise and fund housing associations to provide affordable homes to those in housing need. They are obliged to eliminate racial discrimination and promote equality of opportunity. The grant system facilitates the use of private sector finance and thereby increases the number of homes that associations can provide for a given level of government grant.

The Federation of Black Housing Organisations provides advice to Black groups on setting up specialist housing co-operatives and associations. It has also encouraged the development of schemes which help housing organisations achieve racial equality and provide trained professional housing personnel from the ethnic minorities.

The National Federation of Housing Associations monitors all new lettings made by housing associations through its national Continuous Recording System (CORE), which includes data on the ethnic origin of households. In Scotland, this data is also recorded through the Scottish Continuous Recording System (SCORE) and the Scottish Homes Own Stock Recording System (SHORS).

The Housing Corporation

The Housing Corporation has a statutory duty to promote good race relations. It supports housing associations established to meet the needs of ethnic minority people and managed by a committee of which at least 80 per cent are from the ethnic minority communities.

The Corporation's ethnic strategy for the five-year period to 1996 envisaged:

—investment of about £750 million in ethnic minority associations to provide new homes;

—increased revenue grants to assist ethnic minority associations to become independent;

—the transfer of about 2,400 homes from established associations to ethnic minority associations;

—ownership or management of 16,500 homes by ethnic minority associations at the end of the five-year period; and

—the establishment of training programmes to assist the associations to reach required standards of performance.

Housing Advice

Housing advisory centres have been established throughout England and Wales since 1970 by local authorities and voluntary organisations. The Department of the Environment has produced booklets on housing law affecting private and public tenants. Translations of some of the booklets are available in Bengali, Gujarati, Hindi, Punjabi and Urdu.

Codes of Practice

The Code of Practice in Rented Housing is a statutory code drawn up by the Commission for Racial Equality and approved by Parliament. It is applicable in England, Scotland and Wales and covers all areas of rented housing provided by local authorities and other public sector landlords, housing associations and co-operatives, and private landlords. The code explains race relations law and provides guidance on avoiding discrimination in access to housing, quality and service delivery.

The code states that housing organisations should:

—review regularly all their practices and procedures to ensure that they do not discriminate directly or indirectly;

—keep ethnic records of tenants and applicants and monitor them on a regular basis; and

—provide all staff with training and guidance on the equal opportunity policy.

In 1991 Parliament approved a similar statutory code for owner-occupied housing. Applicable in England, Wales and Scotland, it covers all agencies, organisations and individuals involved with non-rented housing. They include estate agencies, lending institutions, local authorities, solicitors, valuers, surveyors, property developers, and vendors and purchasers.

The CRE also produces advisory guides on aspects of race and housing.

Racial Harassment

Efforts have been made by local authorities to deal with problems of racial harassment on certain housing estates. Initiatives have included:

—producing publicity about the issue, and about help available, in ethnic languages;

—using injunctions against perpetrators of racial harassment;

—improving incident monitoring systems, particularly in relation to the ethnic origin of the victim;

—planning the introduction of emergency support for victims, such as telephone helplines and reporting centres; and

—bringing statutory and voluntary agencies working on racial harassment together in multi-agency panels.

Hostels and Other Social Housing Projects

A number of hostels have been established by voluntary organisations for young Black and Asian people who have left home or who are homeless. Most are financially supported by central or local government. The growing number of elderly people among the ethnic minorities, particularly from the Asian communities, is also receiving attention. A number of social, recreational and sheltered housing projects run by voluntary agencies and local authorities have been established, as well as special schemes such as home helps and domiciliary meal services. A training scheme for voluntary workers with these elderly people has been introduced under the Government's Helping the Community to Care programme.

Through the efforts of Scottish Homes, housing associations and local ethnic minority groups, a range of housing projects have been set up in Scotland to meet the needs of the elderly, single homeless and victims of domestic violence.

Relations between the Police and Ethnic Minorities

The subject of police relations with ethnic minority communities received close attention after civil disorders which occurred in 1981 and 1985, particularly in London and Birmingham. The report of the inquiry into the 1981 disturbances (see Further Reading) said that these could not be fully understood unless they were seen in the context of a complexity of political, social and economic factors. It emphasised the dilemma for the police of how to deal with a rising level of crime while retaining the confidence of all sections of the community. Commenting upon the 1985 disorders, the then Commissioner of Police for the Metropolis (London) referred to the social context in which they occurred as economic deprivation, high levels of unemployment, high rates of crime, and a sense of injustice and discrimination. To gain the confidence and co-operation of the ethnic minority communities, a number of initiatives were introduced by the police service. These included measures to increase recruitment of police officers from the ethnic minorities, improved training for police recruits, the formation of community relations departments, and policies for tackling racial harassment.

Police Recruitment and Equal Opportunities

There is widespread agreement that the composition of police forces should reflect the society that they serve. The reluctance of members of the ethnic minorities to join the police service has been a cause of concern for many years. At the end of 1994 out of a total of 127,290 police officers in England and Wales, 2,100 were from ethnic minorities, about 1.6 per cent as against 1.5 per cent in 1993. The highest rank held by an ethnic minority officer was that of Chief Superintendent. On the other hand, a much higher proportion of London's Special Constabulary (volunteer police officers who perform police duties as auxiliaries to the regular force) are Black or Asian. The number of people from the ethnic minorities recruited to the police service has been rising in recent years. In 1993 4,885 police officers were recruited, of whom 193 (4 per cent) were from the ethnic minorities, a slightly higher proportion than in 1992. In addition, a number of police forces are taking positive steps to give ethnic minority applicants a more equal chance of selection. A Black Police Association in the Metropolitan Police has been established that will act as a support network for ethnic minority officers and civilian staff.

All police forces in England and Wales have:

—developed and published equal opportunities policies;

—drawn up grievance procedures relating to police and civilian staff;

—developed some form of monitoring scheme; and

—embarked on structured training programmes.

Forces in Scotland have also developed equal opportunities policies and training programmes.

Annual statistics submitted by forces contain detailed information on the ethnicity of police and civilian staff. HM Inspectorate of Constabulary uses this information to encourage forces to look critically at their selection, appraisal, postings and promotion procedures in order to remove artificial barriers to equality of opportunity. Minimum height requirements and upper age limits for candidates have been abolished, widening the range of potential recruits.

In 1992 London's Metropolitan Police Service published a training handbook for all recruits entitled *Focusing on Fair Treatment for All* as part of its equal opportunities training.

Police Training

A specialist unit, run by an independent training company, provides training organisations such as the Bramshill Police Staff College and police forces with practical help and support in community and race relations training. The unit's tasks include the instruction of police trainers in community and race relations, and the provision of a central bank of training material for use by the police. The unit also promotes contributions to police training from outside, lay, contributors. The Scottish Police College provides courses at all levels of police training, including race relations and awareness of ethnic issues.

Community Consultation

The Police and Criminal Evidence Act 1984 requires arrangements to be made in each police area in England and Wales for obtaining the views of local people about policing, and for securing their co-operation in preventing crime. These arrangements have been reinforced by the Police and Magistrates Courts Act 1994, which has introduced a duty for police authorities to consult the community on policing plans. In Scotland these issues are dealt with by the Justice Charter published by the Scottish Office. Almost all areas have police/community consultative groups which discuss issues of local concern.

Efforts are made to develop relations with young people through community liaison work in schools and youth clubs. Lay visiting of police stations has been successfully operating in a number of areas, and is an important element in securing greater public awareness of how people who have been arrested are treated by the police.

Racially discriminatory behaviour by police officers is an offence under the Police Discipline Code. Allegations against the police may be pursued through the independent Police Complaints Authority or through the courts.

Tackling Racial Harassment

The Government is committed to the elimination of racial harassment and believes that it is vital for the police, working with other agencies, to provide an effective and co-ordinated response to racial incidents.

In the light of official reports by the interdepartmental Racial Attacks Group (see p. 27) and the House of Commons Home Affairs Committee, the Government has emphasised that there should be a clear and well-publicised commitment by police forces to tackle racial incidents as a priority by reassuring potential victims and deterring potential harassers. Most forces publish multilingual literature stressing how seriously they view such incidents, and encouraging victims (particularly repeat victims) and witnesses to report them. Senior officers are responsible for overseeing racial incidents and policies, while some forces have specialist race relations departments. The monitoring of the police response to racial incidents has been stepped up by HM Inspectorate of Constabulary. The Crown Prosecution Service (CPS) has guidelines on racially motivated offences. It has been agreed with the Association of Chief Police Officers that the police should mark files of cases of racially motivated attack before passing them through to the CPS.

The Media

Broadcasting

The radio and television organisations—the BBC (British Broadcasting Corporation) and the commercial companies licensed by the ITC (Independent Television Commission) and the Radio Authority—aim to reflect the diversity of cultures and languages in British society and provide programmes of interest to all sections of the community.

BBC guidelines for programme-makers stress the need to avoid unnecessary reference to race or racial origin, to ensure objectivity and accuracy in the coverage of racial questions and to guard against stereotyped images. The ITC programme code also includes requirements relating to race and religion.

Television

The BBC has produced a variety of multicultural magazine and documentary programmes for television. They include the topical award-winning documentary series *East* and *All Black*; *Network East*, an arts and entertainment magazine; *Bollywood or Bust*, a Hindi film quiz; a *Bookmark* trilogy on best-selling Black writers; *Africa Summer* series, including documentaries, films, literature, traditional music and politics; and *Sadhus—India's Holy Men*. Plans to increase the range of multicultural programmes were announced by the BBC in September 1995.

The concerns and interests of the ethnic minorities have

also been the subject of programmes made by the commercial television companies. Channel 4 in particular has shown a commitment to multicultural programming in the popular arts, in fiction and in journalism. Examples of its programming have included *The Black Bag*, a current affairs series for Black and Asian communities; *Story of a Community*, charting the settlement of the Bangladeshi community in Britain; *The Great Maratha* series, broadcast in Urdu and Hindi; and an Asian drama serial, *Family Pride*. Channel 4 screens Indian feature films regularly.

The number of cable and satellite television channels licensed by the ITC that target ethnic minorities in Britain is growing.

Under the Broadcasting Act 1990 and the BBC Agreement religious broadcasting must not contain abusive treatment of the religious views and beliefs of others.

Radio

Local radio is playing an increasing part in ethnic minority broadcasting. A large proportion of BBC local radio services broadcast programmes for ethnic minorities, with a mix of local news, views, information and entertainment. For example, BBC Radio Leicester and Radio WM (West Midlands), which both provide regular programmes for ethnic minority listeners, launched a combined 18-hour-a-day Asian network in autumn 1996.

There are 180 independent commercial radio stations, ten of which are 24-hour ethnic services owned and operated by the minority communities which they serve. These are:

—five stations for Asian listeners: two Sunrise Radio stations (one for Greater London and one for Bradford), Sabras Sound in the East Midlands, Radio XL in the West Midlands and Asian Sound in East Lancashire;

—two Choice FM stations for the Black community in Birmingham and Brixton, London;

—a Turkish and a Greek service, both in Haringey, London; and

—a multi-ethnic radio station, Spectrum International, covering Greater London.

Cable and satellite radio stations for ethnic minorities include Radio Orient for the Arab and Muslim community, and Sunrise Radio-Europe for Asian and other minorities.

Employment and Training

The BBC is committed to promoting equal opportunity in employment and training, and is taking positive action to equip ethnic minority candidates to compete on their merits and thereby increase their representation in the BBC workforce. Such initiatives include work experience schemes and training opportunities in journalism and broadcasting production techniques. The BBC has also set ethnic targets to be achieved by the year 2000. The targets and the achievements reached in 1994–95 in network television and radio, regional radio and the World Service are set out in Table 11 below.

The CRE has encouraged the establishment of media access courses for ethnic minority people.

Table 11: Proportion of Ethnic Minorities Employed by the BBC, 1994–95 *Percentage*

	1994–95	Target (2000)
London		
Network TV	8.3	8
Network Radio	6.3	8
World Service	12.9	8
Regions		
Scotland	1.0	2
Wales	1.3	2
North	3.8	4
South	2.0	4.7
Midland/East	5.0	6

Source: BBC Annual Report and Accounts 1994–95

The Press

A number of publications are designed specifically for members of the ethnic minorities. Such titles, in English and other languages, are generally published weekly, fortnightly or monthly, although the *Asian Age*, the Urdu *Daily Jang* and the Arabic *Al-Arab* are dailies.

The *Asian Times* and *Eastern Eye* are English language weeklies. The *Sikh Courier* is produced quarterly. Established Black Caribbean newspapers include *The Gleaner* and *The Voice*. The Voice newspaper group also publish *The Weekly Journal* and *Pride* magazine. The weekly *Caribbean Times* also covers African affairs.

The number of Black and Asian journalists working on provincial and local London newspapers has increased over recent years, though fewer are found in the national press.

A code of practice agreed by the newspaper and magazine industry says that the press should avoid 'prejudicial or pejorative reference' to a person's race, colour or religion, and that it should avoid publishing such details unless they are directly relevant to the story. The code is enforced by the Press Complaints Commission, whose membership is drawn from newspaper and magazine editors as well as people from outside the industry.

The Arts

The last 20 years have seen growing official recognition of ethnic minority arts activities as an important aspect of contemporary British culture. All Regional Arts Boards in England have a policy of reflecting cultural diversity in their areas, as have the national Arts Councils (see below).

Financial help for ethnic arts is given mainly by the Arts Councils, by local authorities and by the CRE.

Arts Councils

A wide range of arts activities is undertaken by Britain's diverse communities, covering both traditional and new forms of artistic expression. In its support for cultural equity, the Arts Council of England funds:

—Black and Asian dance and drama;

—training schemes, including arts administration and technical skills;

—wide-ranging tours of writers from Africa, Asia and the Caribbean;

—music (including touring circuits promoting the music of Africa, Asia and the Caribbean); and

—Autograph, the Association of Black Photographers, which produces a monthly newsletter and has an exhibition programme and a picture agency featuring the work of Black photographers.

In addition the Council helps:

—the Institute of Visual Arts, which explores new internationalism in the visual arts through exhibitions, publications, lectures and seminars; and

—the African and Asian Visual Artists Archive Project, which collates documentation from exhibitions of work by artists of African and Asian origin, and provides a resource for students, curators and researchers, and a base for producing new educational materials.

The Council, together with the Regional Arts Boards, also supports agencies which are helping to develop an infrastructure for Black and Asian arts across England.

The Scottish Arts Council (SAC) has adopted a policy to ensure the full participation of members of minority ethnic communities in the arts. To help implement this policy the SAC:

—publishes a leaflet in several Asian languages setting out the Council's aims and activities;

—gives priority to ethnic minority arts projects; and

—holds a database of minority ethnic artists and organisations.

The Arts Council of Wales gives grants to community organisations, including ethnic minorities, to help with the costs of promoting arts events. It also supports, together with the Welsh Office and the local authorities, two of the leading arts organisations in South Wales: the Cardiff and District Multicultural Arts and the South Wales Intercultural Community Arts.

The Commonwealth Institute

The Commonwealth Institute is the educational and cultural centre responsible for promoting the Commonwealth in Britain through exhibitions, collections, educational programmes, publications and information. It provides country and regional displays on the Commonwealth countries, arts and crafts exhibitions by Commonwealth artists, weekend and holiday workshops, literary events, pupil programmes, conferences and symposiums, in-service teacher training, curriculum packs and booklets, and a Resource Centre, which includes a Literature Library.

The Institute is currently funded by the Foreign & Commonwealth Office. Through the need to make it more self-financing, the Institute launched a Vision for the Future strategy in 1993 designed to carry it through to the 21st century. The strategy comprises an upgraded Educational and Cultural Centre; revitalisation of the Commonwealth Galleries, including a new *Wonders of the World* exhibition (which opened in 1996), displays on the Commonwealth regions, and a global information and communications centre; and a Conference and Events Centre.

Ethnic Arts Activities

Prominent theatre companies include Tamasha, Black Mime Theatre, Talawa Theatre Company and Tara Arts. ADiTi is a national resource organisation for South Asian dance. Adzido Pan African Dance Ensemble, Union Dance, Shobana Jeyasingh Dance Company and JazzXChange are leading dance companies.

There has been a growing recognition of the achievements of Black and Asian artists and an increase in the number of galleries featuring their work. African, Caribbean and Asian music now has a broad appeal that is not confined to any particular communities. In addition there is a considerable Black music emphasis—jazz, R & B, Blues and Soul—in the output of two jazz radio stations covering Greater London and the North West of England.

Carnival is an activity which forges strong links between the Caribbean and other communities. The best known of the carnivals in Britain takes place at Notting Hill in London. Inspired by the Trinidad Carnival, the Notting Hill Carnival has been described as a combination of community arts, music, street theatre, community entertainment, multicultural celebration and political statement. Celebrated for the 31st time in 1996, it is the largest event of its kind in Europe, attracting well over one million visitors. The Arts Council of England is preparing a national policy and strategy for carnival arts development and is supporting the setting up of a National Carnival Database in order to raise awareness, understanding and profile of this art form.

A one-year postgraduate certificate course on the Asian arts, combining the resources of the University of London's School of Oriental and African Studies and Sotheby's Educational Studies, covers the arts of the Islamic world, China, India, and Japan and the Buddhist world.

Addresses

Advisory, Conciliation and Arbitration Service, 27 Wilton Street, London SW1X 7AZ.

Arts Council of England, 14 Great Peter Street, London SW1P 3NQ.

BBC, Broadcasting House, London W1A 1AA.

Commission for Racial Equality, Elliot House, 10–12 Allington Street, London SW1E 5EH.

Commonwealth Institute, Kensington High Street, London W8 6NQ.

Crown Prosecution Service, 50 Ludgate Hill, London EC4M 7EX.

Department for Education and Employment, Sanctuary Buildings, Great Smith Street, London SW1P 3BT.

Department of Health, Richmond House, 79 Whitehall, London SW1A 2NS.

Department of Social Security, Richmond House, 79 Whitehall, London SW1A 2NS.

Department of the Environment, Eland House, Stag Place, London SW1E 5DU.

Equal Opportunities Commission, Overseas House, Quay Street, Manchester M3 3HN.

Equal Opportunities Commission for Northern Ireland, Chamber of Commerce House, 22 Great Victoria Street, Belfast BT2 7BA.

Federation of Black Housing Organisations, 374 Gray's Inn Road, London WC1 8BB.

Home Office, 50 Queen Anne's Gate, London SW1H 9AT.

Housing Corporation, 149 Tottenham Court Road, London W1P 0BN.

Immigration and Nationality Department, Lunar House, Wellesley Road, Croydon CR9 2BY.

Independent Television Commission, 33 Foley Street, London W1P 7LB.

Metropolitan Police Service, New Scotland Yard, Broadway, London SW1H 0BG.

National Council for Voluntary Organisations, Regents Wharf, All Saints Street, London N1 9RL.

National Federation of Housing Associations, 175 Gray's Inn Road, London WC1X 8UP.

Northern Ireland Information Service, Stormont Castle, Belfast BT4 3ST.

Office for National Statistics, 1 Drummond Gate, London SW1V 2QQ.

Police Complaints Authority, 10 Great George Street, London SW1P 3AE.

The Radio Authority, Holbrook House, 14 Great Queen Street, London WC2 5DP.

Scottish Information Office, New St Andrew's House, Edinburgh EH1 3TD.

Trades Union Congress, Congress House, Great Russell Street, London WC1B 3LS.

Further Reading

Official Publications

Statutes

Race Relations Act 1976.	HMSO	1976

Annual Reports and Statistics

Commission for Racial Equality.	CRE	
Control of Immigration: Statistics, United Kingdom.	HMSO	
Immigration and Nationality Department Report.	Home Office	

Other Official Publications

Black & Ethnic Minority Women & Men in Britain.	Equal Opportunities Commission	1994
The Response to Racial Attacks and Harassment: Guidance for the Statutory Agencies. Report of the Inter-Departmental Racial Attacks Group.	Home Office	1989
The Response to Racial Attacks: Sustaining the Momentum. The Second Report of the Inter-Departmental Racial Attacks Group.	Home Office	1991

Racial Attacks and Harassment. Third Report of the Home Affairs Committee, Session 1993–94. Vols I and II.	HMSO	
Community and Ethnic Relations in Europe. Final Report of the Community Relations Project.	Council of Europe	1991
Measure for Measure: A Comparative Analysis of Measures to Combat Racial Discrimination in the Member Countries of the European Community.	Employment Department	1992
Civil Service Data Summary 1994.	Cabinet Office	
Large Companies and Racial Equality.	CRE	1995
Racial Equality Means Business.	CRE	1995
The Brixton Disorders 10-12 April 1981 (Scarman Report). Cmnd 8427.	HMSO	1981
Education for All (Swann Report) Cmnd 9543.	HMSO	1985
Social Focus on Ethnic Minorities.	HMSO	1996

Index

Printed in the United Kingdom for The Stationery Office C30 6/97 9385 5739